Nan

Poetic greet
in abunuance upon you.

Msgr Thomas Cahalane

Msgr. Thomas Cahalane

The Poet Within

Tomãs õ Cathalãin

Published by
KAN DISTRIBUTING INC.

The Book Team:
Ernie Nedder, Publisher
Tomās ō Cathalāin, Author
Corinne Gay, editor
Sharon Nicks of Types, Graphic Design

Printed in the United States
KAN Distributing

Individual Copies: $10.00
10% from the sale of this book will go to outreach charities.
Ordering Information
From the author: 520-747-1321
Check local bookstores

ISBN: 978-09841716-5-1

DEDICATION

In deep gratitude to my dear parents Thomas and Hannah, for their transparent faith, sincere prayer, enduring faithfulness, commitment, and hard work. In praise and thanks to God for them.

The Stone Circle... Druid's Altar

The picture on the cover of this book gives a view of the author's home neighborhood. The house to the top of the picture center right, beside the tree cluster is the Cahalane household. In the forefront of the picture is the stone circle, a very well known archaeological site in West Cork, Ireland. Before it was excavated in 1957, it was known locally as the Druid's Altar. Carbon dating done in the 1980s established the date of the circle/Druid's Altar to be in the 11th century B.C. People worshiped the unknown god here more than 3,000 years ago.

The circle is made up of seventeen standing stones. It is oriented so that the main axis of the circle (a line extending from the middle of the gap between the entrance portal stones to the center of the axel stone/altar stone) is aligned north-east/south-west so that the sun setting on the evening of the winter solstice shines directly on the axel stone/altar. It is thought that this stone circle was dedicated to sun worship. See the stone circle poem on page 18.

Druids in ancient Celtic Ireland were spiritual leaders, magicians, astrologers, fortune tellers, and healers – who presided over a ritualistic religion centered on the worship of nature deities. The position of ancient Druid or Celtic priests was coveted because the Druids were not expected to fight or pay taxes. Moral philosophers as well as interpreters of the will of the gods, they taught that the soul was immortal and, at death, passed from one person to another. The Druids served as a cohesive force among the Celtic tribes. Their power was eventually eroded by Christianity, which was introduced to Ireland in the 5th century A.D.

FOREWORD

Msgr. Thomas Cahalane came to the Diocese of Tucson from Ireland as a missionary priest. In the midst of the Sonoran Desert his deep sensitivity and poetic spirit grew through his years of ministry. On the occasion of his fiftieth anniversary as a priest he has published his collection of poems written on many occasions through his life. They are a delight, some moving, some whimsical, some deeply personal. They were written for a wide range of occasions and will touch your heart.

A priest enters the lives of people in many different ways. Msgr. Tom has shared the joys and sorrows of the people he continues to serve. He has been deeply involved in their lives and their struggles. His poems reflect the heart of a true shepherd who knows his people. He has a wonderful way with words and captures in a few phrases a world of ideas and emotions.

Msgr. Tom throughout his priesthood has taken time away as the Lord stepped away from time to time. That quiet, meditative time away has afforded him an opportunity to reflect on God, on beauty, on prayer, and the spiritual journey. His poems are ways for us to encounter God.

Msgr. Tom holds a deep love for the beauty and serenity of

his homeland in Ireland and his poems provide an occasion to encounter the Irish soul and spirit. His love of his homeland leaps off the pages of his poems and provide a glimpse into his heart.

Reading through the pages of his collection gives the reader a wide range of feelings and experiences that refresh and delight. Enjoy!

Most Reverend Gerald F. Kicanas, D.D.
Bishop of Tucson

The Poet Within

Each person has a poetic soul and heart. What is important is that we experience our poet within. Words that give expression to our poetry are merely the clothing on its body. Our poet lives within us, beyond all words, in a place that I know to be sacred – that place I know to be God ... hence the title "The Poet Within."

The following selection of poems are gleaned from personal reflections over the years. They are somewhat reflective of my life in poetry. They are dedicated in deep gratitude to family, extended family, staff – (past and present), parishioners, friends, and to all who have been a significant and integral part of my fifty year journey in priesthood. It has been and is a journey of discovery and encounter with the holy through sacred faces and spaces in very ordinary and extraordinary ways.

As I observe this Golden Jubilee milestone anniversary, my deepest emotion is one of humble gratitude for God's amazing and magnificent blessings to me, and through me during these five decades of priesthood. I bow down in gratitude for the flow of God's amazing grace into and through my human experience and frail and vulnerable humanity. In the words of the great hymn *Amazing Grace*, I am deeply aware ... *T'was grace that brought me safe thus far*, and I am confident despite my sometimes faltering steps, that *grace will lead me home.*

The poems shared in this collection are an attempt to capture some of the whisperings and movement of God's spirit ... "The Poet Within" in the experience of this priest. The scripture passages introducing each section have been very seminal portions of God's word to me over the years. The verse from Psalm 16 in the Thursday evening Compline prayer, says it all on how God has blessed me and continues to bless me ... *He has put into my heart a marvelous love, for the faithful ones that dwell in the Land.*

I am grateful beyond words to my parents – Tomas and Hannah, and to my brothers – Con and Michael, who are now all together, hopefully and prayerfully, in the communion of saints. My gratitude flows to my sister Mary, and brothers, John and Pat Joe; to all extended family and friends, who have been, and are a source of God's *amazing grace* to me and with me during this fifty year desert journey. My deepest thanks is anchored in prayer, and hopefully is reflected through the pages of this book ... "The Poet Within"

My special gratitude to all the loving people who have encouraged me through the years to do this book. My heartfelt acknowledgement to Corinne Gay, my assistant, for her loving efforts through many drafts of this book and bringing it into its final copy.

May these reflections for all who read them be a bridgehead leading them to discover the poet, the sacred, the God within. May our God of the creative and poetic eye, open our eyes and heart to see, know and love the poetry of His/Her creation. In the ancient language of Ireland – *Go reib mile mait agat* … a thousand thanks to you.

Tomās ō Cathalāin

CONTENTS

I God & Nature

In the beginning, when God created the heavens and the earth.

Genesis 1:1-2

God said: Let us make human beings in our image, after our likeness. Let them have dominion over the fish of the sea, the birds of the air, the tame animals, all the wild animals, and all the creatures that crawl on the earth. God created mankind in his image; in the image of God he created them; male and female he created them. God blessed them and God said to them: Be fertile and multiply; fill the earth and subdue it. Have dominion over the fish of the sea, the birds of the air, and all the living things that crawl on the earth.

Genesis 1:26-28

God looked at everything he had made, and found it very good.

Genesis 1:31

Poet of Creation

I write a poem,
A poem to the Poet.
To the Poet of Creation.
You look with your poetic eye.

Across the vastness of space
Down the long corridor
Of galaxies of shining orbs
And you gaze upon reflections of yourself.

You gaze with your loving and caring eye
You glance with prodigal care
On the many, many unique poems
Made in your own image.

You are the Poet
We are your poems.
Thanks Poet of Creation
For the poems and poetry of life.

The Table of the Heart

After each poem is penned
There is a feeling of completion.
But then on a deeper level
There is an infinite sense.

An inexhaustible depth
Pulling into limitless space.
The sense of deep mystery
Becomes all-pervasive, all-encompassing.

It embraces with a fullness and wholeness.
It gently draws and nurtures
All reality into a quiet stillness
Into a profound unity.

There is triggered
A hungry longing
To be forever still
At the table of the heart.

Then there comes
The call to celebration.
The feeling of feast,
At the banquet table of mystery.

The food of this transforming, transcending mystery
Fills and expands the appetite of the soul
To a satisfaction that satisfies.
Yet beyond it all is a hunger that rages on.

Grand Canyon Cathedral

The cathedral of this canyon is full of your
awfulness,

Its charity gapes wide open to embrace me,

My soul overflows in a spirit of thankfulness
at the beauty of your communion.

My God, I'm so much alive in you here.

Fill the cathedrals of man with this sense of
your living presence.

Mothers and Canyons

This canyon is vast and wide.

Its beauty is now silent in moon beams,

Like a mother's beauty deep and still
in the moon beams of memory.

Theirs is a depth as deep as this canyon,
and a beauty as grand,

Thank you, Lord, for beauty in mothers
and canyons.

The Creator's Presence

O God, your awful presence pervades the stillness
of the moonlit canyon,

The murmur of the distant waters whispers a gentle
and eternal call,

The trees stand in reverent silence,

The stars glisten with a sparkling attentiveness.

If only man could pause and be still in this night
of beauty

All human hearts would be canyons reflecting the
beauty of your eternal presence.

Cemeteries

Lord, cemeteries are so often sad and forbidding,
yet, they are alive with the living dead.

This morning's snowfall touches and caresses the
eternal silence of their sleep.

It seals their graves with immaculate beauty and
purity.

Lord, if this is only a glimmer of the beauty of
the snow of heaven, bring me and all my friends
to that eternal snowfall.

The Foreverness of Beauty

The tall palm trees
stand watchful guard beside the gravesites
Their stately stance echoes
the staggering beauty of living now dead.

Some of their arms are limp and broken
beneath the burden of snow-clad mystery.
Lord, why does beauty wound so deeply,
hurt so deeply, pain so much?

Is it because your great beauty
breaks through
the limitation of time
and can only live forever in eternity?

If this be so,
thank you for broken and wounded trees
in this cemetery lawn
and for lives wounded in death beneath them.

Waters Celebrate Escape

The ebbing tide
Has gradually receded,
Suddenly it is gone,
Revealing the muddy estuary floor.

Channels meander through the sloppy flat
With fresh waters rushing and racing
From surrounding hills, fields and forest
Having purified the countryside in its baptismal wash.

They have gathered again
Into running and tumbling and singing streams
Creating white-foamed water falls
With varied musical melody.

On the instrument of rocks and rapids
These waters celebrate
Their escape from enslavement
In song and dance.

Then suddenly after freedom's leap
With gliding, sliding grace
They join their parent mother sea,
And are absorbed into the safe-keeping of her bosom.

The Water Fall

The water fall pours and runs
Over the top lip of the crevice.
Then it tumbles and splashes
In white-foamed flying tongues

It plays a symphony of sound
Through craggy lips and uneven teeth.
As its fingers run through
The instruments of stringy rock.

It bellows percussion notes
As it plays and fiddles with the
Instruments of air.
It beats the drum of the whirling pool.

It does so with pounding and relentless blows.
Its stream of music
Echoes on and on
Beneath and beyond the walkway

It shouts its tune of freedom's beat
Beyond the rapid leap.
Then it puts on its dancing shoes
As it trips and steps

Leaps and runs.
It turns and twists
Circles and glides.
It pauses and walks.

Again and again
It twirls its dress of foamy white
And bares its agile dancing feet
To the symphony of echoing sound on nature's stage.

Adrift

The boat is suddenly adrift
Its engine stalled and powerless.
A sense of fear and helplessness
Possess me like the running tide.

The engine starts, splutters and stalls.
Will the drifting boat crash
Or the clear the island rocks ahead?
Help, help, help becomes a desperate call.

A distant boat moves close
But then comes no nearer.
The call for help continues loud-throated
As I eye the anchor.

The distant boat begins to move again,
Is it coming in the rescue direction?
Yes, no, maybe … yes, yes, yes, *yes!*
Relief, release and gratitude are now free flowing.

The rescue line slung aboard
Securely tied within the stalled craft.
Gradually, both boats move toward shore.
Waves of gratitude replace all fear and helplessness.

Throbbing Thundering Friend – The Sea

The engine is suddenly dead
Vulnerability opens wide and deep as the ocean,
Apprehension now my driving force
Grips the oars.

My little boat is drifting out to sea.
I row towards the nearest point of land,
For a brief while – a while that seems forever.
I'm coming no nearer to land.

The sea and wind breathe forth strong sighs
I wonder with a feeling of helplessness
As the sighing breasts of the sea
Grip and rock my little boat upon its bosom.

I wonder – will my friendship
For my friend the sea be overwhelmed
By the waves of night.
I wonder again at my own finiteness

I sigh deeply
As I row frantically
In the absorbing presence, power and majesty
Of my throbbing, thundering friend, the sea.

The Burning Bush

All along the pathway
Are leaves and leaves and leaves
Fallen from the burning bush of autumn
I walk upon their burning fire.

Their flames light up the pathway
As waters from the stream
Sing their own greetings
To this fiery autumn scene.

I walk along the flaming leaf-way
beneath the burning bushes.
The waters rush on white-tongued,
Despite this autumn blaze.

I am embraced and enraptured into the heart
Of this autumn mystery.
I take an acorn spark of fire into my hands
And walk along in the midst of flames.

Like the three young men
In the fiery furnace
I too sing songs of praise
To the God who befriends me in these autumn flames.

I sing with the singing stream,
I dance and run
I slide and glide
With its graceful element.

I do so
In praise and prayer
To my God of the flaming leaves
And the burning bush.

The Blossoming Tree

The blossoming tree
Stands in desert landscape
Its roots beside the living stream
Of the watery dripping hose

It mocks winter's death
In its springtime bloomy dress
Its branches gently dance
They quiver and shiver with hope

The trees elongated narrow stem
Holds its multi-fingered hands aloft
To the domed blue cathedral ceiling
Praying in praise and wonder

It sways and bows
Beneath its burden of mystery
Its crowded flowery fingers
Point with hope to infinite skies

The Flaming Tree

The rustling tree
Stands tall in stately elegance.
Its late autumn changing leaves,
Flutter and dance to the early morning sun.

Its bulk of leaves like large coins
Seem suspended and translucent.
They give high praise, honor and adoration
In their matins prayer to the hidden mystery.

Sparrows swim from tree to adjoining tree
Through the invisible element of wind and air.
While the flaming tree with its golden coins
Adds new intensity to the fire-dance.

Is this the burning bush?
Must shoes be removed on this Holy ground?
An inner gentle voice calls out
… *Come no nearer* … be still and ponder!

Autumn Leaves

The autumn leaves
Are tumbling down in death
From blazing forest trees
In yet another change of life.

The leaves and trees
Symbolize a mystery at the heart of all life,
Like the ebbing and flowing tide,
Death and life are locked in mortal combat.

The dying and dead leaves
Give off a fresh decaying smell,
As they return to the dust of earth
From whence they came.

Then beyond the death of winter
Out of a grave of seeming lifelessness
New life will rise up in spring
And steal away the power of mortal death.

Then the sacrament of Springtime
Will proclaim to all with eyes to see
That yes indeed
Life is stronger than death.

But now the autumn leaves
Proclaim a season of life's journey.
Death is but a passageway
In the cycle of this mystery.

All things both great and small
Will fall as autumn leaves
And rise again in Easter springtime
Where autumn leaves never fall in death.

The Eclipse

A sliver of orange peel shadow
Covers the edge of the full moon.
Gradually its light is dimmed
Its outline declines and disappears.

It is in total eclipse
Its circumference obliterated.
Is this a symbol of human life
At first resplendent in the image of God?

But so often in shadow
Even in darkness,
The Divine Spark hidden
But never extinguished or obliterated!

The rays of the Risen Son
Pierce through all shadows and darkness.
Evil will never eclipse the Risen Son
In the changing sky of life

The Stone Circle

A circle of tall oblong stones
Define a sanctuary place.
For more than three millennia now
It stands in Drom-beag – the little mound.

The stone altar slab
Suggests animal and even human sacrifices here.
An urn with human cremains
Marks the heart of this worship space.

Is this a cathedral dedicated to the sun
Before the Son of God appeared?
Its tallest stones marks the Winter solstice – the suns low point
And makes it perhaps a temple to the Son of all seasons.

The God of nature was worshiped here
Before the God of revelation became manifest.
It is now a place of pilgrimage
Where pilgrims come in searching awe and questioning wonder.

Perhaps this stone circle symbolizes unconditional love
God's sanctuary deep in every heart?
The God whose heart was broken on the cross
Calls all beyond stone circle hearts.

II Beginnings

Call of Jeremiah

Before I formed you in the womb I knew you.
Before you were born I dedicated you,
A prophet to the nations I appointed you.

"Ah, Lord God!" I said,
"I know not how to speak; I am too you."

The Lord answered me,
Say not, "I am too young."
To whomever I send you, you shall go;
Whatever I command you, you shall speak.
Have no fear before them,
Because I am with you to deliver you,
Says the Lord.

Jeremiah 1:5-8

Womb Art

I proclaim with the psalmist,
It was You Lord, who created my inmost self,
And put me together in my mother's womb.
My inmost self is of Your artistic hand.
What marvel, what wonder, what mystery!

The psalmist prays on,
You know me through and through,
From having watched my bones take shape
When I was being formed in secret
Knitted together in the womb.

Lord, You are the master artist.
You work with paintbrush and chisel
On the canvas and marble of mystery.
Is this how You created my inmost self?

Is this why my inmost self
Is always restless except in You?
Are Your artistic pieces of the womb always live creations?
Does each womb-piece carry a non-repeatable copyright?

Is my inmost self as a unique creation
Fulfilled and satisfied only in the Artist's studio?
With the psalmist, I can only ponder and say
God, how hard it is to grasp Your thoughts.
How impossible to count them!
What marvel, what wonder, what mystery!

The Birth Room

The Sacred event of six births
Emerged to fullness of life
In the birth room
Of the place called home.

Many years have passed.
The six infants have grown to adults.
Holy pictures adorn the walls
Now as then.

The thorn-crowned head of Jesus
Hangs beside the birth-bed,
A silent testimony
To the birth-pangs of life.

The birth room shrine
Is mostly silent now.
Shrines are places of reverence
For recalling memories.

They recall sacred events
In the families of persons and nations.
Birth rooms are shrines
Of the sacred beginnings.

A Sacred Bed

I lay upon a bed,
A sacred bed
Where once I was wombed
In the loving embrace of parents.

A bed in the room of my birth,
No other room in all the world
Can be so sacred to me.
I received life here.

I came to life here.
I was nursed to life here,
And now I am here again
At home in the heart of home.

Wondering with a deep sense
Of reverence
For the persons and place
Where I came to be.

Beyond the Birth Room

Returning to the birth room
Is a mystical and transcending experience.
I journey back from the now
To the moment when I was not.

I am filled with a silent awe
Wondering in the depths of stillness
How I came to be,
- how I was loved into life.

This mystical experience
Becomes self-transcending, beyond the now
Beyond my beginning moment
And all moments in between.

I am absorbed in presence,
In the presence of the great mystery.
I am possessed to the depths of my being
Freed from the limitations of space and time.

I am swept into the depths of the eternal now.
I float beyond the time where I was not
Into the infinite ocean
The ocean of the great "I AM."

I think beyond the moment when I will no longer be
And rejoice in knowing that I will forever be
In the arms of the great "I AM"
Beyond the birth room, the death room
and all rooms in between.

Home Into the Earth

To return to our roots,
Is to go home into the earth of our
Total experience.
It is to make bridgeheads.

Bridgeheads across the fractures of our journey.
It is to rediscover the vital
Thread of our beginnings,
And string them through again.

Into each nugget of life's happenings.
Like the giant oak tree
Standing with its massive size
Sustained in its hanging limbs and bark.

In its clawing and grasping roots,
It stands now,
Where once a meager acorn fell
Unnoticed on a little piece of earth.

In all its being the oak tree
Reaches upward from its roots,
And back down into a little piece of earth
To return home is an all absorbing experience.

To Return Home

To return home
Is to be reborn,
To be renewed at the source of beginnings.
It is to recover and rediscover the stuff of memory.

It is to move beyond memory
To place and space
And to sense and live again
Moments once passed.

Moments now cherished and relished
Through the window of nostalgia.
It is to enter into affinity
With what is infinite in the journey of time.

It is to sense
With eyes, ears, taste, smell and touch,
Yes, with one's soul,
What is of home and beyond.

To return home is to be reborn
To deeper conscious depths of life,
And sing a hymn of praise and thankfulness.
In the home-sanctuary place.

Tongues of Flame

Flying sparks explode
Into the darkness of the starry light.
Waves of suffocating smoke
Flood through the welcome doorway of home.

Hungry flames with devouring appetite
Crackle within the confines of the furnace room.
Tongues of flame in angry consuming rage
Leap through the slated roof.

Flames of paralyzing fear
Erupt through happy home memories within.
The flames without
Fuel the flames within.

The tongues of flame within
Speak their own language of terror
- your childhood home
Will soon be engulfed in flames.

The sturdy house of home
Which has weathered the storms of many decades
Looks so weak and vulnerable now
Against the trapped pool of fire hungering to envelope the roof.

Energized by ravishing feelings of helplessness.
Buckets and buckets of water
Are tossed upon the fiery element.
Slowly it quenches the blaze's fiery thirst.

The sturdy house of home with crowded memories
Stands aghast in holy reverence to its past.
It mocks the dying fires
In the midst of the star-studded night.

Vulnerability is My Name

Vulnerability is my name,
More real than my family name,
Pre-dating my baptismal sign,
Crying for its identity in coming to life.

Reaching for sustaining nourishment in its need,
Groping for security, attention, love
In its childhood journey,
Reaching out with risking openness in awkward adolescence

Clinging, growing and
Hurt in relationships.
Experiencing the pain of aloneness,
Loneliness, searching.

Vulnerability is the deep gorge
Of life within me,
Into which and from which flows
The main spring of life.

Vulnerability shall be my name
In Death.
Calling out more fully than before
My identity in gasping, fading, silent breath.

III Family

God's Espousal to His People

I will Espouse you to me forever:
I will espouse you in right and in justice,
In love and in mercy;
I will espouse you in fidelity, and you shall know the Lord.

Hosea   2-22

Other Fields Beyond

You walked the field of human life
Always aware of other fields beyond.
You tilled those fields
That were given you awhile.

You worked from early morning
Years in sweat and toil.
You labored long and hard
In honesty and truth.

But your life always spoke
Of other fields beyond.
This message of you inner life
Is now our guiding star.

You left the field of human life
At the early break of day,
Never saying goodbye,
As you hurried to other fields beyond.

Goodbye is not a word
For those who will meet again.
See you
In other fields beyond.

The High Priestess Breadline

The high priestess
Bakes the bread of hospitality
With care and skill
That betrays a long lifetime.

As she offers the elements in hands
Consecrated by long and loving practice,
Her memory sometimes recalls names and faces
From the hungry multitudes who feasted on her bread.

As she kneads the dough
Round and round,
Through her holy action
She celebrates the Lord's great purpose.

Through her action she responds
To His command
"Give them something to eat yourselves."
Suddenly there is a multiplication.

Her breadline stretches away from many bastibles and ovens,
Across a span of years
Gathering an endless multitude
To eat the bread-cake of hospitality.

A Never Ending Day

You tiptoed off in early morning
Never really saying good-bye.
Your presence was always
A gentle, listening, absorbing gift.

You read life deeply, intently
With the language of the heart.
You sped off to the heart of reality
In the quiet of morning.

Your quiet bigness
Burst forth
Into the brightness of
A never ending day.

"Good-day" is really the word,
Not good-bye,
Until we meet again
In the never ending day.

Double Holy Day

Annually it's a day of graced memories
For the family it is a double Holy Day.
Our parents were called home
Separately and together on September 17th.

So many memories rise up in gratitude.
The distance of the years bring greater clarity,
To a father and mother whose lives were lived
In great faith, hard work, prayer, and care.

Lives not perfect, but persistent
In striving to live the real values.
From the distance of childhood
Treasured memories rise up of the day's end.

The family is huddled together in prayer
Reciting repetitious prayers.
The living room is suddenly a sanctuary place,
The element of mystery and the holy ebbing through.

The holy bond of Communion grows deeper
With the celebration of each double holy day.
The living room of childhood at day's end
Leads us into union in the limitless living room of mystery.

The Cake of Hospitality

The cake of hospitality is baked,
The ritual is performed
With prayerful care and devotion
The dish is cleaned and ready as a chalice.

The flour and sour milk mix
Is blessed and sprinkled with soda.
Round and round the dough is ground
And then into the oven of transfiguration.

The bread of hospitality
Rises in welcome greeting
Its air of freshness and flavor
Smells all through the house.

It's been life-giving
And life sustaining bread,
Feeding a hungry multitude
In family, friends and strangers.

The Holy Mountain

John, the disciple, and his dog
Stand beside the memorial cross.
They are transfixed in skyscape and seascape,
Suspended between heaven and earth.

They stand alone on the holy mountain.
In the presence of the most sacred symbol.
They stand in the company of the holy ones
– The communion of saints … the invisible choirs.

It is a mystical scene
Where the heavenly choirs
Gently push around John, the disciple,
As he gazes around in wonderment and awe.

The faithful disciple and his friend
Descend from the place of the holy cross.
He walks along … alone and not alone
In a quiet, unhurried, contemplative posture.

He walks in faith and faithfulness.
Possessed by the transcendent vision
From the mount of transfiguration.
Possessing an all-transforming vision in the soul within.

God's Gardener

You lived and bloomed in life's garden,
Your care-taking work in God's garden
Was a joy to your soul.
You worshiped the God of mystery there.

In every blade of grass,
Every shrub and plant and flower.
With each shovel of earth,
You dug deeply into the soil of mystery.

You would say –
"My work in the garden is my prayer."
In this you were an ordinary
Yet uncommon mystic.

You worshiped in God's garden
From early dawn to fading twilight.
You did so with all your heart, soul and mind.
With great spontaneity and magnanimity of heart

You loved your neighbor as yourself, within life's garden.
Those who met you in life's garden,
Greeted you as "Big Mick, the gardener"
Or "Big Mick, the gentle giant."

Springtime was your most holy garden season
The daffodils of childhood
Your most favorite flower.
The garden-owner has called Big Mick the gardener home,

To the garden of eternal springtime,
Where the daffodils of childhood bloom on forever.
Gentle giant in God's garden
See you in the other garden beyond.

Mary

On her baptismal day
she was named Mary.
The name given to the God bearer,
embracing the name above all other names.

A sister in a family of five boys,
Mary's life models, her namesake.
Through her prayer, hard work and servanthood
She declares ... *I am your servant O Lord.*

Her life's pattern in prayer, hard work and service
continues in response to God's call in family.
She echoes ... through family ... her namesake's prayer
My soul proclaims the greatness of the Lord.

My spirit rejoices in God my Savior.
The first Mary's prayer
becomes her prayer in family
for he who is mighty has done great things to me.

Through prayer, hard work and loving service
a family is blest through its servant...Mary.
Blest again and again through her servanthood
as sister, wife, mother, aunt, grandma and friend.

God's care and presence
came into the world through Mary.
His presence blesses the small family and the BIG family
through the person ... *whose name is Mary.*

Benjamin Among Us

The Benjamin among us
In the family of six,
Was named after a servant slave boy
And the servant carpenter of Nazareth.

His patron's - Patrick and Joseph
Have guided him from childhood,
To servanthood in life …
… In parenthood, career and family.

Adventurous and persistent as Patrick
Kindly and caring as Joseph,
He moves on land and sea
Securely protected by his patrons.

Joseph's Technicolor coat in the Spirit
Spreads around him in rich blessings.
It maintains his Benjamin profile
Shielding him from snakes without and snakes within.

Family Bookends

The family bookends are now imprinted
with the initials JP and PJ.
They enclose and guard two surviving family volumes.
The names ... John Patrick, Patrick Joseph are bookends

They guard the family patrimony.
helping the in between volumes stand tall.
The bookends and volumes in the family library
await their transport-call to the eternal library.

The parent co-authors of the six volumes
have been transported to their copyright home.
The first the oldest bookend have been transposed
with an in-between book to the eternal library.

The patrons whose name the volumes bear
are translating the contents of the family library
into the mode of eternal email
where family volumes and bookends will be no more.

The Memorial Cross

The memorial cross on the hill
Stands as a holy marker.
Framed against sea and sky,
It points to the infinite.

It is a living reminder of cherished names,
Lives and relationships.
It is the declaration of belonging
To be the holy company of family and neighborhood.

It's in remembrance of a new millennium,
Also in memory of one who bore the archangel's name,
Whose eyes of faith envisioned this marker of salvation
On this hilltop near home overlooking the sea.

The holy marker is universal
Transcending time and space.
Bringing the holy mystery of salvation
Into all times and places.

The cross on the hill
Is a memorial to the Holy One.
The Holy One who died upon it
...That all may have infinite life beyond sea and sky.

Journey of the Heart

A January journey
From sunshine to snow
In geographic and emotional climes.
A journey to a bed-side

In loving prayer and prayerful love,
Touching heart and soul deeply
In their currents and tides
Human and divine.

Spirits tossing their waters
Into flowing and ebbing motions,
Rippling and storming
Upon the shoreline of the heart.

A new journey commences with new birth pangs
From safe harbours
Of handshakes, glances and presence
To limitless space beyond the journey of the heart.

Viaticum Bread

Each day the sick room
Became the supper room.
The desire for earthly food
Decreased as the body weakened.

Appetite for spiritual food increased,
As the hidden self grew stronger.
The spiritual menu became Viaticum.
'Bread for the journey,' said the priest.

'No,' said the hidden self of the guest,
'It's bread for a long journey.'
On the last days
He feasted on nothing more.

What else is needed
If this is the Bread of Life?
On the last day
He spoke 'Amen' only,

To the Host in the Viaticum bread
He then sped off quietly with Him
In the early morning
On the long journey to never ending day.

Death's Call

Death of a loved one challenges us
To look at the meaning of life.
It loosens our grip
On the non-essentials.

It frees us to move
With less baggage.
It calls us to promote,
To live the real values,

Friendship based on love, faith, hope.
Death calls us
To empty our hearts and hands
For what is forever.

Growth and Growing

Our growth and growing is sometimes submersion in darkness,
Like the grain of wheat
Falling into the loneliness of its ground
To emerge out of the soil of its own pain.

To stay in the ground of our own pain
Is to remain as the lonely grain
Scattered atop the surface of human experience
Refusing to be lost in its earth,

Our growth is like tender, sensitive thread-like roots
Of the wheat grain born in its own pain,
Or the strong grasping, clasping steel-like roots
Of the acorn born out of its pain into the giant oak tree.

We too are called to be born, again and again,
No, not born – to be reborn again and again.
Submerged in the darkness of growth and growing
We too emerge beyond death to hope and life and resurrection.

Love Has Many Faces

It greeted me in another's pain at birth,
Cuddling, caressing, and caring for me in my helplessness.
It collapsed the wall of selfish individualism
In my teen and youthful years.

Developing as a force and power within,
Yet reaching out beyond itself.
Love is possessive, hurting, destroying,
Just as it is liberating, freeing, exalting.

In its selfishness it lies, manipulates, pretends,
In its selflessness it is open, vulnerable, truthful,
It can be all of these
In an attractive and hospitable smile.

Yet real love is always ready to suffer
In the discovery of its own truth.
Its true face is furrowed, trusting, patient, caring
Waiting to die in its own pain as it discovers its eternal face forever.

The Seventieth Harbor... *Cuan Na Seachta*

Today I give thanks seventy times seven.
Thanksgiving in never ending motion,
For seven times ten years of life
Around the seventieth milestone birthday

This thanksgiving flows like the ocean
Washing into many shores.
The shores of infancy, childhood and family
The shores of manhood, call, discipleship, mission.

It's been a journey to and from the shoreline
Into the deep in calm and storm
An inner compass gently leading and directing
The fragile sailboat of life.

At times the sailboat seemed so small
Absorbed in the vast ocean of mystery.
The computer of the inner compass
Transcribing and downloading messages from afar.

The daily ongoing download revelations
Are now overwhelmed in gratitude's gigantic waves.
The seventieth harbor of childhood days
Is now the graced harbor of the years.

Home Prayer Room

The prayer room of home
Basks in the stillness of morning.
Swallows dash and dart in prayerful flight
Beyond the window in soaring, floating contemplation.

The clock on the wall
Tick-tocks in pendulum swing.
It marks and recollects in time
The many prayer moments in this sacred space.

So many faces appear in memory
Now crowding the prayer room of home.
Station Masses, daily family Rosary times.
Meal gatherings for family and guests.

This space is truly sacred space,
Where priest and priestess celebrated Presence.
Sacred presence in endless family gatherings
In comings and goings of pilgrim wayfarers.

Now this home prayer-room
Is holy ground in memory
Where the rhythm and rhyme of vocal prayer times
Echo on High with the swallow and the ticking clock.

IV PRAYER

A Song of Ascent

To you I raise my eyes,
To you enthroned in heaven.
Yes, like the eyes of a servant
On the hand of his master,
Like the eyes of a maid
On the hand of her mistress,
So our eyes are on the Lord, our God,
Till we are shown favor
Psalm 123: 1-2

A Soul Thirsting for God

O God, you are my God, for you I long;
For you my soul is thirsting.
My body pines for you
Like a dry, weary land without water.
So I gaze on you in the sanctuary
To see your strength and your glory.

For you love is better than life,
My lips will speak your praise.
So I will bless you all my life,
In your name I will lift up my hands.

My soul shall be filled as with a banquet,
My mouth shall pray with joy.

On my bed I will remember you.
On you I muse through the night,
For you have been my help;
In the shadow of your wings I rejoice.
My soul clings to you;
Your right hand holds me fast.

Psalm 63:2-9

Solitude's Ears

Silence is the ears of solitude.
The inner-ears of silence
Listen deeply to faraway murmurings of the heart.
They are attuned to solitude's land of mystery.

They hear the still, quiet voice within
The voice that beckons us to come apart
And rest awhile – in the source of all life.
Rest, be renewed and recreated.

Noise-pollution … the drumbeat of our age
Drowns out the inner-ears of solitude.
We walk and run and rush about
Deaf to the voices of the inner-ear.

Our living so often on the surface
Enslaves us in compulsive patterns.
We bob and drift on the surface of life's ocean
With no anchors, mooring us to the ocean bed.

Despite the many wavelengths
Turning us onto the information highway,
We can miss the wave-length of the inner-ear
-Connecting us to solitude's highway.

Unless we attune to solitude's inner-ears
We can live both deaf and mute
In a land of perpetual restlessness,
-Never hearing solitude murmurings from the land of mystery.

.

Alone and Not Alone

The call to prayer
Is a call to be alone and not alone.
The Master of prayer leads the way.
He went up into the hills by Himself to pray.

When evening came He was there alone.
Alone and yet not alone,
Alone in dialog listening to Himself!
– No, alone reconnecting with the Father.

Prayer, dialog, and listening to the Father,
Is more of listening than speaking
– Listening to the still deep voice within,
– A voice of gentle loving blessings.

A whispering into the inner-ear.
Whisperings of delight, love, joy and gladness.
Faint clear murmurings
– You are My beloved.

My favor rests on you,
– The favor of My compassion, love, and mercy in abundance.
You are not alone – I am with you.
Alone and yet not alone,
Alone with mystery in prayer and wonder and awe.

The Eyes of Solitude

The eyes of solitude
Scan the inner-world of the soul.
They beam like gigantic searchlights
Across the immense landscape of the spirit.

They are connected to a vast contemplative radar dish
And peer into infinite skies.
They are filled with visions
Of darkness and light, calm and storm.

These inner-eyes are lighthouses to the soul,
– guiding it to its port of call
– guiding it to its safe haven,
Where it is filled with wonder and love sublime.

There it comes to rest, to holy repose
As it gazes in stillness on its love divine.
Then it is embraced in holy union
And is transported beyond itself.

Its eyes of solitude become still in quiet and silent gaze.
The contemplative radar dish stands still in reverent pause
The eyes of solitude
are filled by the sky of mystery.

The Prisoner and the Contemplative

The prisoner and the contemplative
Live in worlds of great similarity
Grill and cloister
High walls and cell.

The doors of the cloister
Are locked from the inside,
The doors of the prison
Are locked from the outside.

Worlds that seem so similar
Yet so different.
Lord, it is all so simple
True freedom comes from within.

You put it so simply
"The Kingdom of God Is within you."
The prisoner can be a contemplative
The contemplative can be a prisoner

Prayer Walk

The prayer walk
Is a journey into a childhood prayer book of memory.
A journey across the pages of childhood
Through the neighborhood by the sea.

At Matins time God turns over the pages,
Beginning with the first in the birth room.
There His word proclaims
Before I formed you in the womb I knew you.

Before you were born I dedicated you.
Walk out with me now into the prayer book of creation.
Open your inner eyes and ears
Let me come to you anew through the gifts of creation.

As I turn the pages, open wide your eyes and ears
See the place where the old school stood,
The school field and each field with its own name and memory.
See and hear the sounds of the ocean.

Listen to the chirping birds, the crying seagulls.
See the church on the hill,
Where you came to know Me in the new revelation
beyond creation
Be still and know that I am God.

The Prayer Candle

I will forever see you in the early morning
Your face caught in light and shadow.
Cast by the burning prayer candle,
Your inner candle fully ablaze.

Communing with your God
Hours before dawn,
Reflected – joy, peace, and delight
On your upturned face.

To this holy moment
You brought your entire day.
From this communing time
The Lord walked with you into the new day.

He filled your broken humanity
With gifts beyond measure.
– Love, peace, joy, hope, and comfort
While always adding new brightness to your faith candle.

This candle
Reflects the light of the Risen Son.
Its light on your transfigured face
Unlike the prayer candle is without shadow.

It is THE LIGHT
Its blazing candle
Forever leading brightly
To the light of eternal day.

Within You – A Hermit

I believe
That within you
There lives a hermit,
Who desires to ponder over

And enter into oneness
With the spirit breathing and brooding
Over the vast spaces and formless mass
Of your inner universe.

A hermit pensively waiting for you
To come away from the journey outward
And let the breathing, brooding spirit
Form landmasses, continents, ocean, and constellations within.

Your hermit, then, with Sabbath rest
Enlivened, possessed and at one with its source
Can journey outward and remake and reshape creation
Against all forces of distracting, darkness
That persistently try to strangle and suffocate the hermit within.

V Priesthood

God's Call To Priesthood

Every high priest is taken from among
Men and made their representative before
God, to offer gifts and sacrifices for sins.
He is able to deal patiently with ignorant
And erring, for he himself is beset
By weakness and so, for this reason, must
Make sin offerings for himself as well as for the people.
No one takes this honor
Upon himself but only when called by God,
Just as Aaron was.
In the same way,
It was not Chris who glorified himself
In becoming high priest,
But rather the one who said to him:
"You are my son;
This day I have begotten you";
Just as he says in another place:
"You are a priest forever
According to the order of
Melchizedek."
Hebrews 5:1-6

He has put into my heart a marvelous love,
for the faithful ones that dwell in the Land
Psalm 16:3

Fifty Years A' Priesting

Fifty years have past
Since the white robed circle of Levites
Processed solemnly into the sanctuary place
There they proclaimed "ad sum …" "… *present*" to the Lord's call.

Prostrate on the floor of the holy of holies
A tidal wave of prayer washed over them.
The company of the holy ones was invoked
Upon their vulnerable and fragile postures.

In the awesome mystique of the Latin ritual
Voices and organ bellowed out …
… *Veni Creator Spiritus* … *Come Holy Spirit*
As the Divine imprint was imposed on each ordinand.

This priestly band of the Order of Melchizedek
was now commissioned …
… to *Euntes docete omnes gentes*
– *Go teach all nations.*

Fifty years a' priesting have now elapsed
Since the commissioning ordination day.
Now there is prayerful pause on the desert journey,
… Towards the land of promise
… The land of mystery so near and yet so far.

Fifty Years Have Passed

As I walk down the class-piece corridor of time,
Fifty years have passed.
Many class-pieces have passed ours,
Which was once the last.

Faces flash from frame and glass.
Reflections of lives lived in faith
Beyond these limitations,
Lives at one time breathing certitude and absolutes.

Perhaps the many empty rooms,
Bed frames and desk frames aimlessly piled
Speak to the shining faces hanging.
"Let us have more emphasis on faith and trust

And less on certitude and absolutes."
And many more empty forlorn rooms and desk frames
And bed frames and class frames
Will hang with life.

Beyond All Intersections

The call to priestly ministry
Is a call to serve at the intersections.
It's a call to be present
At the critical crossroads of life's journey

Often life at the intersections
Is where heaven and hell meet and compete.
Battle is waged there
Between the kingdoms of light and darkness.

In the person of *Alter Christus*
The priest stands in multiple forms of service to mystery.
A service of listening, mediating, reconciling and guiding.
A service of washing, anointing, and feeding the pilgrim wayfarers.

At holy moments of convergence as traffic flows through,
The priest serves in traffic control and mission control.
The light of the world in earthen vessels
Rotates from green to amber to red.

At life's intersections in mission control
the priest manages a wayside inn.
He serves food and drink from the menu of mystery,
Eternal nourishment for the pilgrim's journey beyond
all intersections.

All Nations Inn

The priest, as a person of mystery,
Manages an outlet of a universal chain.
The all nations franchise was founded by a mystery man
Who came to *serve not to be served.*

The all nations inn franchise
Lays claim to extraordinary *quality inn* services.
It claims the founder's spirit and presence
To be among all guests who *gather in My name.*

The staff Baptized Mystery Services Unlimited
Operate all franchise outlets.
They take seriously the words of their founder
... I am with you always to the end of time.

The Inn's restaurant menu is unique.
Offering ... life directions and guidance gifts
Come to Me ... I will refresh you items.
The universal special is always a wonder bread and drink.

The priest as mystery man invokes the presence of the founder
Upon the bread and wine on the guest's table.
The food and drink that perishes not in the eating and drinking
Is consumed with joy, love and delight.

The founder, through his mystery person manager
Gives a universal guarantee to all guests,
"The person who eats this bread will live forever.
... I will raise up on the last day."

Gifts In Return To The Lord

With what gifts shall I come into God's presence
And bow down before God on high?
Accolades of people, budgets managed, designated roles and titles,
People pastored and served, named buildings and portraits!!

Might these be the stuff of upward mobility?
Stuff that can all too easily inflate the false ego
Leading to a bowing down not before God on high,
But before the altar of the false self.

This rather is what God asks of you
Only this: act justly, lovingly, tenderly, mercifully, compassionately
Especially towards the powerless and broken,
"The little ones … the least among you."

Serve Me lovingly, walk humbly with your God
With the true spirit of downward mobility,
Stay in the company of the holy and the holy ones
Avoid walking alone in the company of the false ego.

If you walk in this … My way.
With the stuff of justice, mercy, humility
With these gifts shall you return to the Lord
And bow down before God on high.

Drink My Cup

Can you drink of my cup
– The cup of every Eucharistic moment?
Are you aware of My presence under so many disguises
– In the expected and unexpected?

Can you drink My cup in the
Trust and innocence of little children,
In the aged and the lonely, the married and divorced
In the abused and the abusers?

Can you receive Me in your broken humanity,
As in the wonders of nature;
In the daggers of inner pain and loneliness
As through the singing birds?

Can you meet Me in un-graced as in-graced memories?
Can you welcome Me in rejection and betrayal
As in faithfulness and friendship?
Can you, will you, drink of My cup?

A Sign-Post

To be a sign-post
Never moving – just standing there
Seems so insignificant
So unexciting.

Yet a sign-post
Has as much significance as
The road and roads beyond it.
Faithfully pointing the way
to all pilgrims.

To be a sign-post
Is to stand in a prominent place
Watching people pass by,
Walking, running, racing

Sometimes a few come back
From travel on other roads.
But most travel down
Beyond the sign-post never to return.

Betrayal

The Twin Towers of innocence and trust have fallen.
A hidden unholy war by some of the Lord's anointed
Has desecrated the temple of the Spirit.
Their terrorist acts of betrayal now fully revealed.

A betrayed and wounded people
Meander through the wreckage of trust and innocence.
There are endless questions ...
... How could this be ... how could this happen?

Who can we trust
When the innocence and trust of young life is maimed?
Their Twin Towers suddenly in rubble.
Who can we trust?

So many who should have known
Were under the dark cloud of unknowing.
Suddenly the sun of justice
Shines through the rubble of the Twin Towers.

Rescue workers scramble around ground zero.
Leaders in high and holy places declare zero tolerance-
Healing and rebuilding the Twin Towers
Remains the painful task.

Only the Holy One who was betrayed upon the cross
... Who called out *Father forgive them*
Can heal the brokenness of the victim and terrorist.
Only in God is my soul at rest.

Into your hands, Lord, I commend my spirit.
The prayer of abandonment of the Holy One
Must become the prayer of all who stand helpless and angry.
Out of the rubble we await in hope ... Resurrection and new life.

A Mystical Journey

Fifty years have passed since the journey from
Shannon to Tucson
A page in memory recalls
Goodbyes to parents, family and friends.

Hellos to an unknown future
In a desert place
Unsure yet pretending certainty
In a changing, changeless Church.

Was I ready, prepared
Equipped as a person and priest?
Scarcely! Could I have been? Doubtful.
In the years now passed
I have befriended me as a person

I have come to know God through a stumbling
Faith process of risk and growth
Where faith has become a
Source of personal grace.

Grace has given me a knowing in faith
That the heart of priestly service
Is a profoundly mystical gift
Flowing from the heart of God.

I feel at once abundantly blessed
And yet like a child over-awed
Gazing through the threshold
To the limitless mystery of God.

VI Parish Church

God's Dwelling Place

"Behold God's dwelling is with the human race.
He will dwell with them and they will be his people.
God himself will always be with them.

Rev. 21:3

God is My Portion, My Inheritance

I say to the Lord, "You are my God.
My happiness lies in you alone."
He has put into my heart a marvelous love
For the faithful ones that dwell in his land.

… O Lord, it is you who are my portion and cup;
It is you yourself who are my prize.

The lot marked out for me is my delight:
Welcome indeed the heritage that falls to me!

I will bless the Lord who gives me counsel,
Who even at night directs my heart.
I keep the Lord ever in my sight;
Since he is at my right hand, I shall stand firm.

... You will show me the path of life,
The fullness of joy in your presence,
At your right hand happiness forever

Psalm 16

The Unfinished Church

The unfinished church
Stands as a symbol to the unfulfilled.
It is inviting and uninviting
Like the Bethlehem stable.

Is my life the unfinished church,
The Bethlehem stable?
Does our Bethlehem God
Wish only to dwell within church walls

Or within the unfinished stable of my life?
"He came down from heaven"
To dwell among church walls!
No – "Among us."

From the Bethlehem stable of my life
Does my voice call out amid unfinished walls
In a simple Christmas prayer and greeting,
"Happy Christmas to you."

New Church

Our new church
Welcomes the Bethlehem King.
It embraces all
Who come to hear the good news of great joy.

It's a place of birthing and empowerment
Like the Bethlehem stable.
A place where God's Word is proclaimed,
And His life given.

A love gift from heaven
Given again, again and again.
Do our daily lives recognize His presence
Beyond our new worship space?

In the faces of all brothers and sisters
Whether illegal or friend?
Are our daily actions filled or devoid
Of His all-embracing presence?

Are our happy Christmas greetings
Filled or devoid of hospitality
As we encounter Him beyond our Bethlehem place
In deceptive, stable-like places and faces,

In the street person, the homeless,
In the unemployed, in the refugee,
In all who seek Him
In the sanctuary of human faces?

Open Doors Within

The church vestibule banner
greets, proclaims, and invites...
... All who enter into the holy space
– *Open wide the doors to Christ.*

Are the doors in your inner life ajar or closed?
Ajar or closed in anger, hurt, betrayal...sin?
The one who desires to come beckons you
– *Come to me ... I will refresh you.*

All burdens, bondage, and baggage
which may impede the sanctuary doors of the heart,
must be submitted to the one who desires to enter.
All soul-clutter must be emptied out and abandoned.

Come through the doors of the reconciliation room,
come confess, acknowledge the door-stoppers within.
Come to me, Come to me ...
– Open wide the doors beyond the inner vestibule.

The inner sanctuary will throb and pulsate
with the absorbing presence of the divine guest.
Then the onrush of the holy
will pour through the wide open doors within.

"The Sign"

The yellow poster board sign stands like a lighthouse
in a sea lane of busy traffic.
It's light flashes a loving message ... *Come Home*
to all searching and seeking a secure port of call.

Searchers and seekers who come ashore to inquire
name the lighthouse ..."The Sign."
Its *Come Home* friendly light
causes them to pause and ponder within.

Some come ashore from the storm and shipwreck of life
longing for comfort, direction, healing and wholeness.
The wondering, lost and worn down travelers are invited
to *Come Home* to the house of love within.

The lighthouse keeper
embraces all who come ashore.
They rediscover and *come home* to mercy,
forgiveness, peace and eternal purpose.

The light of the world lighthouse keeper
continues to flash his kindly *Come Home* light
through "the Sign" beside the shoreline of the busy street.
Come home to mercy, forgiveness, peace, and love.

.

The Church Aisle

The Church aisle is a thoroughfare
Leading to the sacred.
Pilgrims travel this way
Through all the changing seasons of life.

They come in endless processions
From birth to death.
They seek encounter with the Holy
Through the living and birthing waters of baptism.

They come down the holy breadline again and again
To be nourished with living bread.
They march along the holy highway
To embrace and be embraced by the Spirit's fire.

The Church aisle welcomes the radiant bride
Ready to meet her husband.
Bride and groom process to embrace the holy in each other.
To recess along the aisle-way in an eternal embrace of friendship.

Broken and hurting seekers come to be reconciled
Hands are anointed and dedicated to servanthood and service.
From this fiery Spirit encounter
There is a sending forth to witness and make all roads holy.

When life departs its fragile dwelling place
It is lovingly brought down the aisle way one last time
To the rituals of water and fire and bread and wine
It is committed onto the resurrection aisle way
Into the procession of endless life.

Christmas-Easter Tidal Wave

The holy Sanctuary space at Christmas and Easter
becomes awash in a holy tidal wave.
God's love becomes tangible
as people wade into the waters of mystery.

There is a profound sense of awe
as the Divine Presence
invades and envelopes the thirsting spaces within.
Hearts are filled with the utter fullness of the Holy.

There are transformations through transcendence
in the healing words proclaimed.
The sacred mysteries overshadow everything
in the language of symbol, story and song.

People feast on the Bread and Wine of mystery.
The onrush of God's living spirit
anoints everyone embraced by the holy tidal wave.
All are led into deep communion.

The holy tidal wave slowly ebbs away.
The Sanctuary space recedes to an empty shoreline.
There is a longing of desire for the waves return,
To kiss and embrace the sanctuary shoreline once more.

Mirror of Easter Faith

The crowds have come and gone,
The empty tomb celebration is past,
The winding sheet
Hangs limp upon the cross.

The Easter Candle
Rises gracefully above its flower bed,
The baptismal pool gushes
With living water.

The once crowded church now empty, is like the empty tomb.
It is full of signs and symbols of the hidden risen presence,
A presence that vacated the tomb to live in you and me.
Are our words and actions signs and symbols,
Revealers, communicators of His risen presence and message?

Can others – living in struggling belief or unbelief,
In darkness or meaninglessness,
Catch a glimpse of the Risen One
In the mirror of our Easter faith?

Or is the winding sheet of selfish ego
Holding us bound
In our own lifeless tomb
Or is our life the Easter Candle?

The Resurrection Rocket

The Resurrection Rocket
Stands poised and pointed
In its sanctuary launching pad.
It symbolizes lift-off.

Lift-off beyond all human finite limits,
Beyond selfishness, pain, evil and death.
Its booster rocket blasted through the door of death
And sped into and across infinite skies.

The Easter Candle looks so helpless now
In this place of mystery,
Yet what it symbolizes
Transcends all helplessness.

It mocks all other
Rocket systems
And laughs and scorns
Their passing fireball power.

All who believe in resurrection energy
Become ticketed passengers on a gigantic ship.
They move beyond gravity force of sin and death
To a new freedom in an endless life.

For now the Resurrection Rocket
Signals loud and clear
'Be ready for lift-off'
To a new freedom place in endless life.

First Holy Communion

It's First Holy Communion time again.
The little children come
in response to the invitation of the Host.
"Let the little children come to Me."

In words strong and bold,
Jesus speaks out in clear language
– Do not stop them for it is to such as these that the
Kingdom of Heaven belongs.

These kingdom people come
with angelic faces and joyful hearts
to take their reserved place
at the Lord's table.

They come as hungry guests to taste the Heavenly Bread
About which the bread-maker says: "If you eat this bread"
You will live beyond your First Communion day
And all communion days, "You will live forever."

He also promises that when the Holy Communion
season of life is over,
– in another season and another day,
the person who eats this bread –
"I will raise up on the last day!"

But for now, it's Holy Communion day.
The angel-face guests
step down the heavenly bread line
and each shout "Amen" to the Living Bread host.

Easter Blossoms ... Springtime Dress

My Lenten winter season is past?
I have been bare and penitential
For many, many days,
Much more than forty days.

For so long I've seemed dead –
To many, a laughing stock –
My hands and limbs empty and bare,
Seemingly lifeless in winter's death.

Now look at my springtime dress!
My spring blossoms
Proclaim new life.
They signal Easter life.

Soon my hands and limbs will be full
And bending with ripe fruit from my penitential days.
There will be plums and plums aplenty
For hungry birds and pilgrim people.

Pilgrim people! Will others notice
The blossoms of your penitent season?
Will they see new fruit
In bending limbs and caring hands?

As the blossoming plum tree in the church Placita
I shout my springtime message in my Springtime dress.
Will you shout yours –
As a Springtime – resurrection – Easter people?

The Oasis Place

The baptismal pool
Is almost hidden within the holy ground.
Its living, cleansing waters
Symbolize the Lord's living spirit-waters.

Refreshing and renewing waters
Life-giving and soothing waters,
The Psalm proclaims near "restful waters He leads us
To renew our drooping spirit."

As desert pilgrims
He brings us again and again
To this oasis place
And renews our drooping spirit.

Like His pilgrims of old
In the desert place,
He leads us too by a fiery pillar
And feeds us with manna from heaven.

He speaks His word of guidance
And leads us along the right path
He invites us
To be true to His name.

Surely if our answer is yes,
Even a struggling and suffering yes,
His goodness and kindness will follow
All the days of our lives.

In the Lord's own house shall we dwell
Beyond this baptismal pool and oasis place.
And yes, He calls us
To live in His house forever and ever.

Church Sanctuary Harbor

The church space is crowded full
God's people in every nook and cranny of the bay.
The sanctuary harbor is full
Brimming over with the presence of the Holy.

The harbor basin is heaving full
With the ebb and flow of Divine Presence.
People are prayerfully absorbed and afloat
In the gentle all-embracing enfolding presence.

The waters of *love divine*
All love excelling,
Joy of heaven, to earth has come down.
Imparting grace and mercy all around.

The tidal waters of the Spirit
Heave with the fullness of the Divine Breath
Breathing life, hope and joy everywhere,
Leading to a deep resting in the Lord of the sanctuary harbor.

Transcendent fullness and wholeness is alive here.
Flowing into the inner harbors of hungry and thirsting hearts.
The Spirit flows into every nook and cranny
Of souls a-thirsting for the living God.

"Quinceañera" Time

Fifteen years have passed
Since birth and emergence to life.
Life as pure gift always evokes thanksgiving.
Hence the Quinceañera celebration.

The young lady comes to the temple
To present herself in thanks, prayer and praise.
It's a time of thanksgiving to the life-givers
To God, parents, padrinos, and la familia.

She comes and stands on a new threshold
Peering into the landscape of her young womanhood.
The gift of who she is offered back freely,
To God from whom all blessings flow.

The mother of the God-bearer
Had her Quinceañera announced by an angel.
With all Quinceañera maidens she proclaims
My soul proclaims the greatness of the Lord.

VII Pilgrims & Pilgrimage

A Pilgrims' Prayer

I rejoiced when they said to me,
"let us go to the House of the Lord."

And now our feet are standing
Within your gates Jerusalem.

Jerusalem, built as a city,
Walled round about.

Here the tribes have come,
The tribes of the Lord,
As it was decreed for Israel,
To give thanks to the name of the Lord."

Psalm 22:1-4

The Need of God's Blessings

Unless the Lord builds the house,
They labor in vain who build it.
Unless the Lord guards the city,
In vain doe s the guard keep watch.
It is vain for you to rise early
And put off your rest at night,
To eat bread earned by hard toil -
All this God gives to his beloved in sleep.

Psalm 127:1-2

Old Friary Ruins

The old Friary ruins stand in silent witness
To a community of pilgrim friars.
The roofless cloister, the tall walls, the splendid arches
Speak eloquently across centuries of time.

A visiting pilgrim group
Meander through this blest space in holy wonder.
They try to visualize this space in all its glory
– its worship, its chant, its prayer, its song.

A tidal wave of desecration,
– the spirit of evil swept through this space.
Plundering and pillaging the holy of holies,
Stealing the holy vessels and books.

The friars were hunted down and murdered.
The desecrated holy space used as a stable.
The plunderers tried to silence the voice of the ages.
But still the pilgrims come harkening to the voice of mystery.

Is the stuff of the friars' faith…
Different from the faith of the visiting pilgrims?
A faith tested and buffeted by trial and tribulation
Is a faith at home in this roofless cloister.

It is a faith with tall walls and splendid arches
Rising to the praise and glory of God.
It speaks eloquently and mystically
Through the friary ruins of all generations.

The Famine Monument

The starved boy in the Famine monument
Stands knocking at the door.
He stands and stares with a dying hope
That the door to life will open wide.

His desperate, emaciated posture speaks eloquently
For voiceless, countless millions.
Millions who knock at a closed door.
– A door shut tight by selfishness, greed and sin.

The starving boy depicts man's inhumanity to man
– Famine time in the human spirit.
He stands alone for the lonely millions
Who starve to death outside the locked door.

The dying boy in the Famine Monument
Symbolizes the Diaspora of a people.
Fleeing with a vague and dying hope,
Fleeing across the vast bowl of tears.

They fled in coffin ships in search of a new world.
For the some who survived
Their children's children come as pilgrims.
They stare in stunned and uncomfortable silence at the
starved boy.

Dominus Flevit ... The Lord Wept

This sanctuary place
Marks the location
Where the Lord wept.
He unburdened the heart of God here.

He looked across the Kedron valley,
The temple in all its glory stood out.
Close by is the place where Abraham offered a sacrifice,
Outside the wall is an execution place.

He proclaimed in tears
If only you had known ...
... the path to peace this day ...
... but you have completely lost it from view.

Does God weep over our global city today?
Is His path to peace *lost from our view?*
Are we failing to recognize
His time of visitation?

Will nuclear enemies encircle us?
... Pen us in
And press us from every side?
Or will our eyes be opened to His path?

God unburdens His heart with love
Upon the global city of Jerusalem
His love encircles us and presses us from every side.
Will we know and view his path to peace this day?

Iona Abbey . . . Holy Space

People meander through the old abbey.
Pondering, gazing, pausing from hidden depths within.
They look, they look in stunned wonder and awe.
Almost overcome by Presence.

The inner appetite is awakened
From hunger within.
It gasps and pant
For the food of mystery.

Footsteps enter into prayerful movement
Sometimes stalled still in reverence.
There is a transcendent lightness of foot
in this encounter with holy ground.

The sacrament of holy space
Becomes all embracing,
Flooding like a river
Into the dry and parched heart.

Might this be a place
Where the hungry heart calls out
Create a new heart within me O Lord,
Renew within me a steadfast spirit.

The Good Shepherd

The good shepherd is fully given to his calling.
His every move and action
Expresses care, sensitivity and a gentleness.
Sheep, dogs and shepherd are bonded as one.

Each collie, each sheep, has its own name.
They are treated with true reverence and respect.
In turn, they know and reverence their shepherd.
They know and listen to every variation of their shepherd's voice.

The shepherd releases bouncing, dancing collies
Into the fog shrouded mountain in search of the sheep.
There is wonderment in waiting, searching eyes
– Peering at the fog enveloped mountain.

Suddenly the flock of sheep appear
Zigzagging through the fog, down the mountain.
The collie races in a semi-circular motions around them,
Ever so gently leading them to the shepherd.

The shepherd calls each of them by name.
They know him, he knows them.
There is transparent security, trust and safety,
As suddenly there is one fold and one shepherd.

Waterford Crystal ... A Holy Shrine

Fire, water, and breath
Tame and shape the formless molten mass.
The creation of the world is staged in miniature.
The divine artisan continues His work.

The divine spark is aglow,
In the furnace of Waterford cut crystal,
Through artistic pieces made in the creators own image
and likeness.
They shine forth in their eyes, minds and hearts.

In a graced partnership,
Between the artists and the divine artisan,
Slowly, carefully and deliberately
Shape and form is breathed into the new creations.

Each finished piece is shared in a cooperative effort.
Flawed pieces are cast back into the molten furnace
To be purged, cleansed and purified.
The creative process begins all over again.

This place of Waterford crystal is a holy shrine,
To God's creative power.
Where His creations sparkle and glow
In transparent and diverse shapes and forms.

Pilgrims to this shrine reverence the Divine Artisan
In the creative work of human hands.
– Creative work vaguely reflecting the infinitely priceless creations
Made in the image of the Divine Artisan.

Reluctant Simon

Simon the stranger was pushed
To help Jesus in His helplessness.
He took your cross beams
To your place of torture, execution and death.

Now a community bearing His name
Do the same for Him, present in the homeless and rejects.
Those treated as refuse and street trash by so many
Are treated with dignity, care and compassion by Simon.

So often those pushed into service
Are reluctant Simons.
The push of your inner inspiration
Takes them beyond their selfish selves.

You open their eyes to see
Beyond the wrappings.
You open their hearts
To embrace you in your *via dolorosa*.

The cross beams of addiction are now
For so many the instruments of torture, execution and death.
You are not abandoned as you lie on the park bench or on the
shellmex arcade.
Simon and the Samaritans are present tending to your needs.

Jericho's Road

London's Strand thoroughfare in this late summer evening
Is a flowing throng of humanity,
It is alive with the music of hustle and bustle
In horn blowing cars and bus squealing brakes.

Shining taxi cabs ferry their well dressed occupants
Off to venues of elegant dining and culture.
The street homeless are almost invisible
Like wild flowers in humanity's garden.

God's voice speaks through them.
He calls out ... *Forget me not ...*
Among your many daily pursuits.
I am present among and within the forgotten ... forget me not.

As you drive about or walk about
Acknowledge me with a kindly gesture.
– A smile, a listening ear, a cup of cold water
To one of *the least of these is done to me.*

Is the Strand thoroughfare Jericho's Road,
Where the homeless lie lost beside the roadside?
The vast busy throng hurry on by, except for the few
Who feed them with crumbs of compassion from
humanity's table.

The Station

It is station time again.
The house is prepared
For the visit of the King.
It's the station Mass season.

The station commemorates another season
A nearby roadway bears its name.
Carraig An Afráin …
– The road of the Mass Rock.

People gathered then in the secret Mass Rock place
To worship and profess loyalty to the outlawed King.
In great thanksgiving the house is now ready
To welcome the King of the Mass Rock Road.

Priests and people who gathered during the Mass Rock season
Risked their lives for the King of kings.
The well prepared home welcomes them in memory,
Lest priest and people forget the season of the Mass Rock Road.

VIII Holy Places

Prayer of a Pilgrim

How lovely your dwelling
O Lord of hosts!
My soul yearns and pines
For the courts of the Lord.
My heart and my flesh
Cry out for the living God.

Psalm 84:2-3

Holy Ground Enclosure

The monastic cemetery
Lies hidden in an obscure corner.
It's a quiet and unpretentious place.
Simple crosses mark fifteen grave sites.

They bear an economy of words.
Occupants names and years of life-span.
R.I.P. and date of new birthday,
Nothing more ... but simplicity and quiet repose.

Its holy ground enclosure,
Walled in by a tall hedge of evergreens.
Together with a resurrection plant
They declare life and mock death.

The monks in this holy cloistered place
Are in deep contemplative repose.
Their long silence merely a prelude
To the alleluia chorus of resurrection day.

Glendalough … Paradise Lost

Could this be the valley of paradise lost?
Perhaps – a vague representation.
Everywhere there are signs and symbols
Pulling at the outer and inner eye to pause … be still … ponder.

The ruins of the ancient monastic city
Stand as stunning testimonials to this holy sanctuary space.
They speak volumes about our pilgrim roots.
About these who came here to feed the hungers of the heart.

The Spirit still pulls us into this holy valley
Whispering into the inner ear.
"Be still and know that I AM God."
You stand and walk on holy ground.

Be a pilgrim – not a visitor or tourist.
Do not let your life end up like empty ruins
Filled with vague and passing things.
Be still … be still.

In this valley I will lead you to your heart
where I will speak
Come pilgrim … pause … be still … ponder
Feed full on my mystic food of wonder and awe.

Sidewalk Altar

Give them something to eat yourselves,
Jesus said to his anxious disciples.
The preacher in the vast cathedral
was proclaiming the same message.

The scattering of people within
were absorbing and reflecting on the words.
In the square outside a few people
were feeding the hungry homeless ... living the words.

On this Sunday morning
where was Eucharist being celebrated?
Who were the celebrants
doing the holy action?

Was God present only
at the altar in the sanctuary?
Or was he equally present
on the altar of the sidewalk?

Was the holy food of God's compassion
present only at the holy bread line within?
Or was it more tangible in the Simon workers
in their communion with the street homeless?

Lourdes ... Feminine of God

Lourdes ... a holy place
Where earth and heaven meet.
Magnificent in peaceful beauty
Where rivers of light and prayer are one.

The grotto and its cave
Throb with tranquility and awesome presence.
Pilgrims hungering for the Holy
Stand, sit and kneel transposed in ecstasy.

Here the feminine of God
Embraces all her children.
She bathes and washes them
In soothing and healing grace-fountains.

She welcomes all who long for the home of love
All who are burdened and broken in body and spirit
Receive her motherly embrace.
She enfolds them gently in the mantle of her care.

The greeting of the angel and now her children
Echo here in song, prayer and praise -
– The simple refrain
Ave, Ave Maria.

Cnoc Muire

The pilgrims come with eyes of faith wide open.
To Knoc (Knock) Muire – Hill of Mary – a Holy Place
They are "still" like the weaned child on it's mother's lap.
Full of trust and confidence in God's maternal care.

Pilgrims rest their weary and burdened hearts
At the abundant breasts of the motherhood of God.
Consumed by a holy longing like the pilgrims of old.
They have journeyed to the holy place.

With the pilgrim's prayer alive in their hearts
I rejoiced when I heard them say
Let us go to God's house.
Now our feet are standing in your holy place.

There around the holy tables
The Mother of the Holy One silently gestures …
– there is your guidance in the holy book,
– there is your nourishment on the table of the Lamb!

Be faithful like Joseph.
Be open to receive me as did John.
The pilgrims are transposed beyond themselves
Contented and at rest in the company of the holy ones.

Corrymeela by the Sea

Corrymeela … a house of Reconciliation by the sea,
A place dedicated to healing and to hope.
A place for building the future in peace.
Is this a dream, illusion, or reality?

The tribal warfare engulfing this northern land
Makes Corrymeela an island in a stormy sea.
It's a safe and shared space
For the weary and fearful to find shelter.

They come to share their troubled stories,
To listen to each other.
They come to build bridges
Where trusting relationships can grow.

They come to see reflected in the seascape
What is so often mirrored in the inner landscape,
– The changing winds and tides, the calm and storm, and currents
That ebb and flow within the tribal ocean.

They come to connect with the Master Sailor
The one whom the winds and sea obey.
They come to know that with Him all winds and tides
and hateful currents
Can be negotiated from this Corrymeela house by His sea of love.

Precious Distraction

Lord – I have come apart to be with you.
I brought my little agenda,
– Little things I want to do.
You distract me from them.

Your whispering inner inspiration beckons me ...
I want you in my company.
Be attentive, be still, be quiet.
Let's be ... just be ... ponder ... be still.

I am more than a distraction
I am your possession ... your possessor.
I am much more,
I am your creator, savior, Lord ... lover.

You are precious to me
Don't you know I have died for you,
I've really laid down my life for you,
And I'm your distraction?

– You take me so lightly!
– Like ... take me or leave me!
Lord, through this time apart you teach me
I am precious in your sight not your distraction.

Santa Rita Solitude

The Santa Rita landscape
Is alive in its autumn dress.
The feast of many shades of green
Fill the pilgrim eye with delight.

The eyes of the soul
Peer beyond the hills, mountains and valleys.
They are drawn into the mystical core
– The core of solitude.

Suddenly a helicopter intrudes,
Desecrating the silent solitude
In this grand sanctuary place.
Its noise pollution is all pervasive.

Is this an omen of things to come?
Will the compulsive addictive drives of our culture
– The "for cost" motive, scar, rape,
and desecrate this sanctuary place?

Will the uninterrupted sounds of silence
Continue to sing creations hymn of praise here?
Will the eyes of the soul continue to feast
On the quiet, still center of its mystery?

Sounds of Solitude

The Sonoita landscape pulsates with mystery
Revealing mystical whisperings in the gentle breeze
The sounds of solitude are all pervasive.
All is still in the sounds of silence here.

The book of creation is wide open,
Its sacred pages full of mystical language.
The sacred author embellishes each chapter
With unrepeatable art forms.

The pages of this sacred book
Flutter with mystical messages and revelations
Its art forms are iconic and sacramental,
Opening up windows to a mystery so near and yet so far.

A sense of contemplative transcendence
Envelopes the heart in wordless wonder here.
It's a sanctuary place of holy solitude
Full of icons and doorways to the holy.

Ode to the Old Yellow School House

Your memory now outlives your oldest pupil,
You stand still reflecting on the journey of many years.
You have withstood the winds and rains
Of a century and three score years.

You stand in desolation, your walls broken
You stand beside the road, your rooms and playgrounds empty.
So many shoe-clad and shoeless feet
Came patter, patter through many years of mornings

Again at each day's end
You sent them forth upon the road
That has led them down
The long, long road of life.

Now and then a few return
And come down the empty road
And gaze into your soul through your windows
Recalling days of childhood.

Then suddenly
Many memories come alive
And sing a song,
Ode to the Old Yellow School House

IX Christmas

So all went to be enrolled, each to his own town.
And Joseph too went up from Galilee
from the town of Nazareth to Judea, to the city
of David that is called Bethlehem, because
he was of the house and family of David, to be
enrolled with Mary, his betrothed, who
was with child. While they were there, the time
came for her to have her child, and she gave
birth to her firstborn son. She wrapped
him in swaddling clothes and laid him in
a manger, because there was no room for
them in the inn.

Luke 2:3-7

Our Stable God – Our Table God

The Lord of the stable scene
Each day becomes the Lord of the table scene.
The God of the stable
Becomes the living bread of the table.

He laid in a manger,
A feeding place for animals,
Now from the table
He feeds His hungry flock.

His birth in a stable
Is an astonishing mystery.
His presence as food on the table
Is an even greater mystery of faith.

How do we proclaim our God of the stable,
Our God of the table?
In a moment of worship ritual
Or in the daily ritual of life!

Our God of the stable becomes our God of the table
So that HE may dwell in the stable within.
His word tells us clearly
"The kingdom of God is within you."

Message From on High

"Peace on Earth"
A message from on high
Celebrated each year for
More than 2000 years.

The Earth of our lives
Has for many decades now
Remained at once open
And closed to this gift.

The Earth of our experience
Is sometimes saturated completely
With its absorbing transforming power
Peace – God's peace on Earth.

Then so often
Our Earth can be uninviting
Closed, hostile unloving
A no man's land.

Across whose landscape rumbles anger
And the forces of violence and war
They ravish the only sacred ground
Into which Peace on Earth can fall and take root.

A Sacred Bowl

The Christmas scene is set
In the family infant bathing bowl,
It is a manger of life
Human and Divine.

The Bethlehem scene
Transfuses this sacred bowl of memory.
The sacred meets the sacred here
As angels proclaim Glory to God in the Highest.

The bathing bowl
Becomes holy now in a new way.
It embraces and is embraced
By the Holy One who dwells among us.

Does the Holy One
Who was born on the first Christmas
Dwell among us
Or within us?

Within us
If our hearts are open like the bathing bowl.
Among us
If we recognize Him in the powerless.

May the Holy One be born anew
And make our hearts His bathing bowl.
May He live among us
In the powerlessness of our Christmas scene.

The Manger Scene

The manger scene
Sits beneath the altar.
The Bethlehem star
Hangs brightly in the sanctuary sky.

The red poinsettias
Proclaim the bloody future of the newborn.
The light-clad trees
Shine forth newborn hope.

The worship space
Sometimes full
Most often empty
Is alive with the magic of mystery.

Camel riders
Journey from afar,
Seeking, searching, hoping to share
Their treasures with the Treasured One.

We are now the camel riders
Following the Bethlehem star of faith.
May our Christmas journeys
Lead our poor tired hearts

To the Treasured One
So that we may share
His priceless love gifts
With all seeking, searching camel riders.

Desert Shield of God

The Desert Shield of God
Comes in helplessness and vulnerability.
Born once as a helpless child in the hillside cave
On the edge of town.

He comes now, again and again,
In the shield of mystery.
He brings into the desert of our hearts
The armaments of love, forgiveness and peace.

The rich fuel of His grace
Beneath the heart's desert floor
Is discovered, reserved, protected and recovered
Through these love gifts from His arsenal.

May the Desert Shield of our Bethlehem God
Send forth again His peace army ... proclaiming
"Glory to God in the high heaven
And peace to His people on earth."

Christmas Homecoming

Our Christmas God
is a God of family.
A God on journey from heaven
To Bethlehem, Nazareth, Jerusalem and beyond.

Christmas time releases our pilgrim God
From the virgin's womb,
Into the womb of the world's hillside cave.
God in Jesus comes into the womb of family.

Christmas is forever,
A homecoming time for family,
To ponder and wonder homecoming
to the womb of mystery.

Its mystique, message and person
So often calls us from empty tombs
To come wander home,
To the holy cave of family

May this Christmas time
Bring all pilgrims safely home.
Home to the God of family and mystery
Who comes home to us.

Ponder and Wonder

Mary pondered and treasured
All these things in her heart.
The things said of her Son
By angels from on high.

The pondering treasuring season is here
What will we ponder?
What will we treasure?
Will we ponder the treasure of the Holy One?

Will our pondering and treasuring
Be more than tinsel and wrappings?
Will we ponder the Divine Treasure
In the swaddling clothes wrappings?

Will we ponder friendship
Human and divine?
Will our gifts – giving and receiving
Reveal what is pondered and treasured in the heart?

Ponder and Treasure

The season of ponder and treasure
Beckons our heart space to be a
Place for God to be born again
A heart-home for the Treasure Divine.

In this season of wonder
What gifts am I pondering?
Will my giving and receiving
Be touched by the wonder of the shepherds?

Will the greetings on the cards
Be greetings to ponder?
Will the wrappings on the packages
Conceal or reveal the Divine Treasure?

What will we ponder and treasure?
Will there be room in the heart-inn
To ponder the Treasured One?
Or will the space be otherwise occupied?

Mary pondered and treasured
And placed the Holy One
In the swaddling clothes of her heart.
To embrace the Holy One.

Does my heart bear a sign
"No room in the inn for Wonder Divine!"
Or does it have pondering clothes
To embrace the Treasure Divine?

Bethlehem Cave Within

Jesus came into our bankrupt nature.
By coming down from heaven.
His birth in Bethlehem's cave
Was His entry into our helplessness and powerlessness.

God of the heavens and the earth
Put on the clothes of our weak human nature,
Jesus deemed equality with God,
Something not to be grasped at.

He came and dwelt amongst us.
Christmas is not a past event.
Christmas marks the beginnings of the promise,
I am with you always to the end of time.

Will this Christmas reassure us, reconnect us
To the Divine's presence with us always?
Will we welcome the Divine Presence
Into the Bethlehem cave within?

Does the evil, the greed and anger of Herod
Still push Him to the margins of Bethlehem's town?
Is there "no room" for Him at the heart of the global village?
" … No room" for Him and His way in the cave of my heart?

Will the Divine Guest be the welcome guest in my Bethlehem cave,
… In the cave of the global village this Christmas?
Can I say, will I pray,
Come Lord Jesus, Come!

The Divine Migrant

Christmas time is the feast of the migrant...
– The Divine Migrant crosses the boundary from heaven to earth.
Jesus did not deem equality with God
something to be grasped at.

Rather He emptied Himself and took the form of a slave
being born in the likeness of man.
Jesus ... the Migrant, became helpless and powerless
in crossing the border between divinity and humanity.

He came down from heaven
and dwelt amongst us.
He migrated from heaven to earth
so that we might migrate from earth to heaven.

Christmas is the feast of borderlands and boundaries
It calls us to meet and embrace the Divine Migrant
in each other and especially in the stranger.
We are all migrants on the move.

As we cross borders and boundaries ...
In our migrant holy meal we pray ...
– *may we come to share in His divinity*
who humbled himself to share in our humanity.

As we celebrate Christmas may we welcome the migrant Jesus
across the borderlands and boundaries without and within.
May we travel securely with His divine passport
into the land where boundaries and borderlands are no more.

Christmas – A Bankruptcy Feast

Christmas is a bankruptcy feast
… the bankruptcy feast of Jesus.
He did not deem equality with God
something to be grasped at.

Rather, He emptied Himself
and took the form of a slave,
being born in our likeness
in the bankrupt cave of Bethlehem.

Bethlehem is God's unambiguous declaration
of Chapter 11 reorganization.
He shed the clothes of His divinity
to enter into the bankruptcy of our humanity.

From the helplessness of Bethlehem
to the shame and bankruptcy of the Cross,
obedient to the legal counsel of the Father's will
Jesus has led us through our human bankruptcy.

Because of this,
God highly exalted Him,
moving Him and us out of bankruptcy
into infinite riches and endless life.

Christmas – War on Terror Season

Christmas is war on terror season.
God's response to all war, hatred and evil
Is through the timeless gift of his Son…
… Jesus who came among us and remains with us.

God's omnipotence disguised in our humanity
Appeared as a helpless child in the Bethlehem stable.
He desires to enter the cave of all terror stricken hearts.
Through the nuclear energy of his love.

Angel voices still proclaim
The way to the future . . .
… The good news of great joy
Is the way of Jesus not the way of Herod.

Whose way is winning the war on terror
In the cave of the human heart?
Will we trust in the non-violent ways of God's love
Or the weapons of violence, war and mass destruction?

Christmas beckons us to pause and to ponder!
Will we make room and welcome for Jesus and his way
In the cave within during this holy season,
… His war on terror season?

The Birthing of God

The humanity of God had its beginnings
in the womb of the handmaiden.
Mary, did you experience morning sickness
during the first trimester?

God of the heavens and the earth
became fully clothed in our humanity,
through His powerlessness and helplessness
as an embryo developing and growing to infanthood.

Joseph, did you rush Mary off the donkey
because of the intensity of her contractions
to the stable-maternity room?
Was she fully ready as you lay her on the floor of the stable?

Were you anxious and afraid with her
as she began gasping and panting in labor?
As midwife, did you marvel as you saw the little head appear?
Did you wonder if this was the birthing of God?

Did you untie the life line cord
and place the newborn at his mother's breasts?
Did you both weep for joy
as the little one nursed tenderly and contentedly?

Christmas is the feast of the birthing of God.
It calls us to the bosom of Love Divine.
There to nurse tenderly and contentedly
on the milk and food of Divine love.

Bethlehem – The Separation Wall

It is Bethlehem time again,
The season of joy and good news.
The joy and good news of Emanuel,
God with us.

In Jesus, God broke down the separation wall
Between divinity and humanity.
"He came down from heaven
And dwelt amongst us."

In the town of His birth,
There is a new separation wall.
It snakes its way through the Bethlehem people,
Creating walls of division, fear, mistrust.

Separation walls of division, fear, mistrust
So often exist within our hearts,
The Bethlehem place where God
Desires to be born and dwell.

As we come to the season of great joy,
Will we remove all separation walls within?
Or shall they snake their way around
The Bethlehem place within??

Spread Bethlehem Everywhere

Christmas is Divine Revelation time.
It is God coming in human wrappings,
In a state of total helplessness
To witness with love.

It is incarnation time
God making His home in our humanity
Befriending our woundedness and vulnerability
Through His birth in the stable.

He came unto His own
And His own received Him not,
But as many as received Him
He gave them power to witness with love.

To witness with His love,
As brothers and sisters
To brothers and sisters
Is to spread Bethlehem everywhere.

His dwelling among us with love
Calls us to trust and abandonment.
Will you, during this Bethlehem time, open the heart stable
So that He may witness with love in you and through you?

Bethlehem ... How Far?

In years ... 2000 years
In miles ... journey to infinity.
In mystery ... so near and yet so far
Nearer than your heartbeat.

Nearer than your breath.
No farther than neighbor.
Bethlehem can be everywhere
It is every place and space.

It is of time and eternity
It is God made man.
It is incarnation mystery
Coming and dwelling and staying among us.

God makes His cave among us and within us
In broken and divided hearts,
In bankrupt and foreclosed hearts.
In hearts yet open, searching, desiring, and trusting.

Bethlehem embraces us into transcendent mystery.
Bethlehem is not so far.
It is always near
Nearer than years and miles and times.

Blessed ... Visitation Time

Before the Bethlehem birthing of God
Old pregnant woman – Elizabeth
Proclaims to her teenage pregnant cousin ...
"Blessed are you who believed."

Believed what or who?
... "That what was spoken to you
By the Lord would be fulfilled."
It is blessed visitation time.

Christmas is a blessed and blessing time,
It is a visitation and embracing time;
Pregnant cousins Elizabeth and Mary
Visited, blessed and embraced each other.

In visiting, greeting and embracing each other
Their wombed infants "leaped for joy".
Elizabeth proclaims to the teenaged mother to be
... "Blessed is the fruit of your womb."

May our messages, greetings and embracings
During this Christmas visitation time,
Make us leap for joy
In the Bethlehem womb of God's love.

High Angel Season

This is high angel season.
The angel said to Mary
… Do not be afraid
… You have found favor.

The angel also said to Joseph
… Do not be afraid,
… To take Mary into your home.
What is your fear now?

So often fear with its many faces
Can put a lock on the door of the heart.
The message from on High is clear
Do not be afraid.

You, too, have found favor through faith and grace
Let the Divine Pilgrim into your home,
The home of your heart.
Unlock the door for Emmanuel.

Emmanuel means … God is with us.
What a mystery to ponder,
Do not be afraid,
Ponder in wonder … Emmanuel.

Prepare the Way

A voice crying out in the wilderness
… *Prepare the way of the Lord.*
John's voice still cries out,
It rings and echoes across the ages.

In this preparation time for the Divine Birth
The Baptist voice calls across the inner wilderness,
… The desert of the human heart,
… *Make straight His paths.*

Make straight his way to the inner core,
To the inner cave of the heart.
He comes in spirit and fire
As He came upon Mary, John and the Apostles.

Prepare the way, prepare the way
He comes in weakness and helplessness.
Every crooked way will be made straight
Every mountain and hill of pride will be made low.

May His birthing in the cave of our weakness
Come from our simple, prayerful invitation
… *Come, Lord Jesus, come,*
Come, Lord Jesus, come.

Bethlehem Y2K

Are you spiritually Y2K compliant?
Is your inner network up and running,
Or are you on a crash-down mode?
Are the doors to your heart's inner modem shut tight?

To become totally compliant,
Open wide the door to Christ.
Invite and acknowledge Him as Lord and Savior.
Let Him lead you into the great jubilee year.

He came into Bethlehem's cave 2000 years ago
So that our inner cave may be taken beyond its crash-down mode.
Tap on the repentance, forgiveness and conversion keys,
Your Bethlehem Y2K mode will be up and running immediately.

You will be spiritually compliant
For the great Christmas event.
Jesus will bring you beyond the threshold
And beyond all millennium jubilees.

The screen on your spiritual Y2K
Will proclaim the timeless message,
– A message to and beyond all millennia:
Glory to God in the highest,
Peace to His people on earth.

Awake! Awake!

It is now the hour for you to awake from sleep.
From the sleep that closes the eyes of the heart.
Now is the time to open them in hospitality.
To recognize God who comes in powerlessness.

The wide open eyes of the angels and the shepherds
Recognized omnipotence in bondage in the manger.
The pagan kings also saw and believed.
Yet – He came unto His own and His own received Him not.

Do we as His own today recognize Him
Beyond rituals, holy words and prayers?
Are our inner eyes wide open
Recognizing and welcoming Him in every face?

If not, it is now the hour to awake from sleep,
From the sleep of selfishness, spiritual blindness – sin.
Then with the inner eyes of the Spirit wide open
The Bethlehem vision of angels and shepherds will be ours.

May we then, with our new shepherd eyes go in haste
And join the angel chorus proclaiming:
Peace, peace, peace, on earth,
On the earth and hearth of every human heart.

X Sabbatical Reflections

The apostles gathered together with Jesus
and reported all they had done and taught.
He said to them, "Come away by yourselves to a
deserted place and rest a while." People were
coming and going in great numbers, and
they had no opportunity even to eat.
So they went off in the boat by themselves
to a deserted place.

Mark 6:30-32

Sabbatical Time

The heart of Sabbatical
Is the call to be alone
In the presence of the great mystery.
It is ultimately a call to solitude.

A call to quiet stillness
A call to listen to the language
Of sacrament in the endless gifts
Of creation and new creation.

It is a call to spacelessness
Beyond all signs and symbols
It is an experience of transcendence,
Wholeness, fullness, otherness.

It is to rediscover the anchors of the heart
Are lodged firmly and securely
On the ocean bed of mystery
And not on mirage or passing shadows or fake appearances.

The heart of Sabbatical
Is feasting the deepest hungers
Of the restless heart
In the food of mystery.

Sabbatical time is a call time
To feast, to celebrate, to know
The enrapturing, possessive and freeing embrace
Of the eternal lover God – Father/Mother

Sabbatical Scattering Time

It's ending time again
Saying goodbye seems so final.
Deeper levels of feeling
Mock what is on the surface.

The eyes of faith look beyond
And bring all things into a new wholeness
Even though it is sabbatical scattering time
There is a spirit bond linking us

To an invisible communications network
That holds us together at the heart of reality.
There is poignancy, sadness and
Hope too in this scattering.

New sources of enrichment and vision
Have build us up for the call to serve.
Deeper contact with the inner self is realized.
A time of quiet prevails, as thanksgiving envelopes the heart.

A call to live out of this heart prevails
A call to see grace in all things
Significant and insignificant
In all things great and small.

Out of Sabbatical Spaces

I am airborne again
Out of Sabbatical places.
The gigantic aircraft
Is crowded with heart memories.

Memories of celebrating faces
And caring places.
Memories of children
And grown up children.

Celebrating life caringly
And lovingly, in friendship,
In prayer, in song, in story,
In shared graces, and hospitable tables.

The flight is weighted down
With memory baggage,
Some glad, some sad, some intimate
Some remote – all evoking and provoking

Deep heart stirrings from the place of mystery.
Yes I am airborne again
Burdened and thrilled
With memories of the heart.

Sabbatical Acorn

I picked up some acorns
In a cemetery place
On the final day of my Sabbatical.
Are these Sabbatical acorns?

They look helpless and lifeless
In a helpless and lifeless place,
Perhaps they only seem so,
They carry deep within them the spark of life.

The Sabbatical season
has gifted me with new acorns,
With potential to be giant oak trees.
Will I nourish them to life?

Will new oak trees of the Spirit
Take root in Sabbatical soil?
Will spirit acorns
Disappear into the wounded soul soil?

Will they spread their strong steel-like roots
Into the ground of being.
Like a giant oak tree in the Spirit
Grown tall from Sabbatical acorns.

XI Miscellaneous

But we hold this treasure in earthen vessels,
that the surpassing power may be of God and
not from us. We are afflicted in every way,
but not constrained; perplexed, but not driven
to despair; persecuted, but not abandoned;
struck down, but not destroyed; always carrying
about in the body the dying of Jesus, so that the
life of Jesus may also be manifested in our body.

2 Corinthians 4:7-10

Graduations

Many years have passed
Since my first school graduation.
No ceremony, procession, party, or goodbye,
From the country school down the road from home.

Years later I discovered such a passage is a graduation.
Then again high school graduation
… No ceremony, procession, party,
But goodbye among peers.

Then a halting "yes"
To a whispering voice
To serve the Lord
To Carlow '57-'63.

Then there was graduation
Through laying on of hands in ordination,
A procession, a ceremony, a party
And many goodbyes.

To a desert place 1963-2013
A new passage – called reality – life,
Endless graduations in personal
Growth, response and service

The call of the whispering voice
Now leads to Golden Jubilee time
And on to more graduations
Before the final graduating call.

Graduation Time

It's graduation time again.
The procession forms and names are called.
Slowly the line proceeds
To the diploma point.

It's one more step
In the long procession of life.
Another stepping away from a nurturing womb
Into a world of new risks and challenges.

From the womb to the tomb
Life is a series of gradations.
The first graduation is
Into the world of helplessness.

Then an endless series of graduations
Brings us to take-charge
For one brief moment
In the in-between-time.

Suddenly we graduate
Through the door of death.
Is this the only real graduation?
All of us are now in a long procession.

Sooner or later each name will be called.
The Diploma-Giver forewarns us,
"Be you always ready
For you know not the day nor the hour …"

There are two kinds of diplomas;
One inscribed with the words,
"Come you who are blessed,
For I was hungry and you gave me to eat …"

The other diploma will say,
"Depart from me you evil ones
For I was hungry and you gave me not to eat …"
For now it's graduation time

The procession is forming
For the final universal gathering.
Slowly the line proceeds to the diploma point
When your name will be called.

The Arsenals of Nations

The destructive power
Stockpiled in the arsenals of nations
Can in a moment
Uncreate the world.

Resources to destroy
Are carefully planned, maintained and protected.
They are cared for and nurtured
Like unborn children.

God-like respect is given them
Because of their fearsome destructive force.
They stand in the landscape of modern times
As cathedrals beckoning worshipers.

To reverence at their false idols.
They fly the skies and plumb the deep.
They scar our landscapes with ever-ready death,
In a world shaped by a God of life.

The Olympic Torch

The Olympic torch
Is raced across the world.
Runners bear its fiery flame
With a graced and passionate sense of urgency.

It finally enters the gigantic stadium
To the welcoming cheers of the vast crowd.
There is wonder and awe in the ritual
As the flaming torch ignites the Olympic fire.

The run of the Olympic torch,
Symbolizes another universal runner and light.
This torch-bearer proclaims
"I am the light of the world."

He proclaims his followers to be torch-bearers
"Your light" in the Olympic stadium of life
"Must shine before others
That they may give glory to my Father."

True glory, not passing glory
More than, much more than, passing fireworks and
the Olympic fire.
There is true glory, wonder and awe
In the universal torch-bearer igniting His fiery furnace of love.

Jesus, our universal torch-runner
Invites us to run with his fiery flame.
We are to run with a graced and passionate sense of urgency
And compete in the stadium of life with hearts aflame.